Festive Blocks FOR A Mega Christmas Quilt

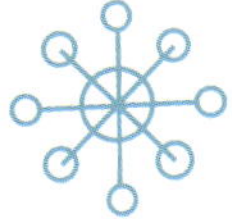

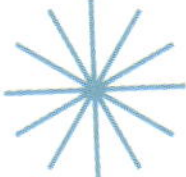

Festive Blocks for a Mega Christmas Quilt

Landauer Publishing, *https://landauer.foxchapelpublishing.com*, is an imprint of Fox Chapel Publishing Company, Inc.

Project Team
Editorial Director: Brian Hurley
Acquisitions Editor: Amelia Johanson
Editor: Christa Oestreich
Designer: Wendy Reynolds
Proofreader & Indexer: Jean Bissell

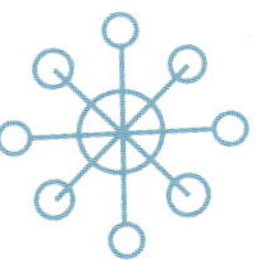

Shutterstock used: Dmitr1ch (wood background: front cover, back cover); Jukov studio (garland: front cover)
Designed by Freepik: 2, 5, 7, 8, 9, 10, 13, 14, 18, 36, 37, 39, 41, 44, 45, 47

ISBN 978-1-63981-170-0

The Cataloging-in-Publication Data is on file with the Library of Congress.

To learn more about the other great books from Fox Chapel Publishing, or to find a retailer near you,
call toll-free at 800-457-9112 or visit us at www.FoxChapelPublishing.com.
We are always looking for talented authors.
To submit an idea, please send a brief inquiry to acquisitions@foxchapelpublishing.com.
Or write to:
Fox Chapel Publishing
903 Square Street
Mount Joy, PA 17552

Printed in China
First printing

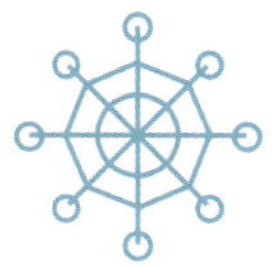

Festive Blocks FOR A Mega Christmas Quilt

25 TRADITIONALLY PIECED DESIGNS

Tracy Perks

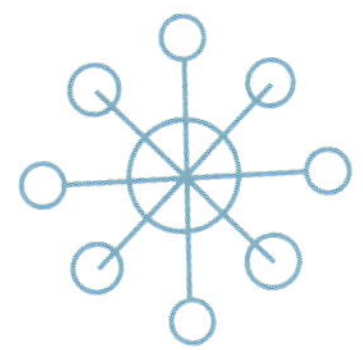

Landauer Publishing

TABLE OF Contents

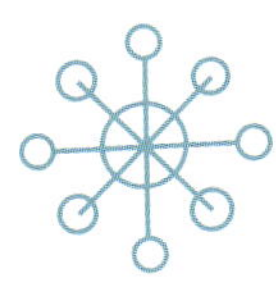

Welcome!

Christmas is a season of warmth, tradition, and creative joy. For me, it's about embracing humble pleasures, gathering memories, stitching something beautiful, and filling my home with festive cheer. This booklet is a blend of all those things. Inside, you'll find a Christmas quilt pattern designed to be flexible and fun along with 25 blocks to arrange as you like, which are perfect for beginners and seasoned quilters alike. But more than that, this is a collection of holiday memories and traditions that make Christmas meaningful in my home.

Growing up in The Valley—a small, rural place with only three streets—Christmas was a time of simple joys. Weeks before, we'd sit with Mum making Christmas baubles for the tree using beads and sequins; each year would be a little fancier than the last.

There was always festive baking in our house. Mum would make the Christmas pudding and Christmas cake weeks in advance. We would all get to stir it, make a wish, and she'd tuck a penny into the pudding for one of us to find on the big day. We'd make mince pies and tiny chocolate truffles as sweet treats.

Looking back, it always felt like it snowed at Christmas. Our dad, a cabinet maker, built us two brilliant sleds. We had the best sleds in The Valley. All these little traditions made the season feel magical.

Now, living on a narrowboat, my celebrations may look different, but the heart of Christmas remains the same: cozy moments, familiar comforts, and the joy of crafting something meaningful.

Whether you're here for the quilting or just a dash of festive inspiration, I hope these pages bring you as much joy as they've brought me. So, grab a warm drink, settle in, and let's create something beautiful together.

Merry Christmas and happy quilting,

Tracy

HOW TO USE This Book

This book is designed to be flexible, festive, and full of creative possibility. You'll find 25 quilt blocks inspired by Christmas traditions, seasonal motifs, and cozy memories. Each block includes row-by-row instructions and can be used on its own or combined with others to create a sampler quilt, table runner, cushion cover, or any project you choose.

The blocks are arranged in a suggested order, but feel free to mix and match them to suit your own style. You'll also find additional patterns for festive home décor projects, including a lap quilt, table runner, and cushion cover.

Before you begin, take a look at the Tools & Materials section (page 10) and the Basic Techniques (page 14). These will help you get started with confidence, whether you're a beginner or experienced quilter.

You can work through the book in order, or you can start wherever inspiration strikes. There's no right or wrong way—just enjoy the process, make it your own, and let the season guide your creativity.

Above: A table runner with a crisp winter design, featuring a snowy tree and candlelight that adds a fresh, modern touch to your festive table.

Left: This comfortable lap quilt was inspired by the classic dessert, Christmas pudding. It's perfect for snuggling under while the pudding simmers and the season settles in.

Right: This cushion depicting a gift tag could be customized by embroidering names in the To and From area.

TOOLS & Materials

Before you begin, here's a list of basic tools you'll need to complete the blocks and projects in this book:

- **Sewing Machine**—Any reliable machine with a straight stitch will do.
- **Rotary Cutter, Cutting Mat, and Quilt Ruler**—Use these important quilt tools for accurate cutting and trimming. I like to use a Creative Grids Stripology® ruler for cutting my squares; it really saves time and improves accuracy. A rotating cutting mat makes trimming half-square triangles even easier.
- **Fabric Scissors and Thread Snips**—Snips are handy for trimming threads while fabric scissors can cut large and small pieces of fabric.
- **Pins or Clips**—Use them to hold pieces in place while sewing.
- **Iron and Pressing Mat**—Pressing is key to crisp seams and neat blocks. Press with an iron onto a pressing mat or ironing board, which will absorb the heat and protect your work surface.
- **Neutral Thread**—Use a good-quality cotton thread for piecing. I like to use Aurifil Cotton 50wt thread for piecing.
- **Needles**—Standard machine needles are all you need for piecing your blocks together.
- **Marking Tools**—Fabric-safe pens or pencils are typically water soluble or naturally erase over time. These are for marking the half-square triangles.

Quilt Rulers
Thread
Sewing Clips
Thread Snips
Rotary Cutter
Cutting Mat

Fabric Requirements

This project is designed to be flexible, so you can use what you have, whether that's a curated Christmas palette, a bundle of fat quarters, or your favorite festive scraps. Feel free to mix and match fabrics to suit your style: traditional reds and greens like I have used, frosty blues and silvers, or even a modern pastel palette. This is your Christmas quilt, so make it your own!

If you're making one of the smaller festive projects (starting on page 36), you'll find specific fabric requirements listed with each pattern.

To make the full 25-block sampler quilt top, the full fabric requirements are below:

- ¾ yard (68.6cm) White ☐
- ⅔ yard (61cm) Gold ☐
- 1 yard (91.4cm) Bright Red ☐
- 1½ yards (1.4m) Burgundy ☐
- ⅔ yard (61cm) Light Green ☐
- ¼ yard (22.9cm) Light Gray ☐
- ¼ yard (22.9cm) Dark Gray ☐
- ¼ yard (22.9cm) Light Blue ☐
- ¼ yard (22.9cm) Brown ☐
- ¼ yard (22.9cm) Black ☐
- 3 yards (2.7m) Dark Green ☐

BACKING FABRIC GUIDE

For a 73" × 73" (185.4 × 185.4cm) quilt, here's how much backing fabric you'll need, depending on the width of your chosen fabric:

Standard-Width Backing (40" [101.6cm])

- You'll need to piece the backing using two panels.
- Each panel should be at least 80" (203.2cm) long to allow for quilting and trimming.
- **Total Required:** 4½ yards (4.1m)

Extra-Wide Backing (108" [274.3cm])

- One panel will cover the entire quilt. No piecing needed.
- The panel should be at least 80" (203.2cm) long to allow for quilting and trimming.
- **Total Required:** 2¼ yards (2.1m)

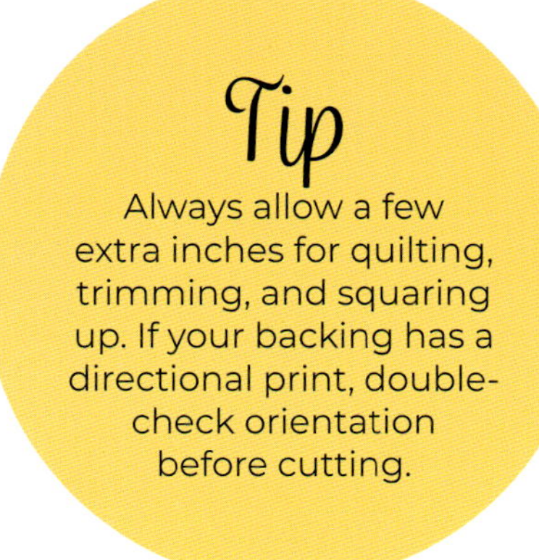

BINDING GUIDE

For the 73" × 73" (185.4 × 185.4cm) quilt, you'll need approximately ½ yard (45.7cm) of binding to go around all four sides, plus a little extra for joining and corners. I used the same dark green fabric for binding as the background fabric on the quilt top.

Tracy's Method:

Cut binding strips at 2½" (6.4cm) wide from a 40" (101.6cm) wide bolt of fabric.

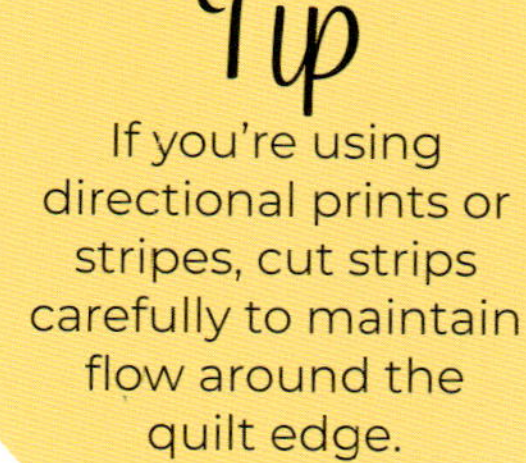

How Many Strips?

8 strips of fabric, with a little bit to spare.

BATTING GUIDE

Batting is the soft middle layer of your quilt that adds warmth, texture, and structure. This layer is where comfort meets craftsmanship, so choose what feels right for your quilt and your season. Common types:

- **Cotton**—Soft, breathable, and easy to work with. Ideal for a traditional feel.
- **Polyester**—Lightweight and holds its loft well. Great for a puffier finish.
- **Cotton/Poly Blends**—A balance of softness and durability.
- **Wool or Bamboo**—Natural fibers with excellent warmth and drape.

For the 73" × 73" (185.4 × 185.4cm) quilt, you'll need a piece at least 80" × 80" (203.2 × 203.2cm) of batting to allow for quilting and trimming.

BASIC Techniques

Before we dive into the projects, I want to walk you through the simple techniques we'll be using again and again. These are the small, steady steps that make everything else feel easier, from cutting your fabric to making neat half-square triangles and preparing your binding. I've broken each part down so you can take your time, enjoy the process, and feel supported at every stage. Once you're comfortable with these basics, the rest of the book will unfold beautifully.

Cutting Instructions

In the sampler quilt, you'll be working with two square sizes throughout. I've broken these into two columns: the first (strips and smaller squares) will be used for piecing while the second (larger squares) is used for making half-square triangles. These measurements refer to unfinished squares, meaning before any sewing or trimming is done.

For accuracy, use a rotary cutter, quilting ruler, and cutting mat. Press the fabric before cutting to ensure clean edges and consistent sizing. All seams are sewn with a ¼" (6.4mm) seam allowance.

Remember that the fabric requirements and cutting instructions for the mini projects (such as the lap quilt or cushion cover) are provided with each pattern.

For blocks, sashing, cornerstones, and borders, you'll need to cut out the following:

Check off when cut

2" × 2" (5.1 × 5.1cm) unfinished:

- White Squares x 51
- Gold Squares x 95
- Bright Red Squares x 136
- Burgundy Squares x 4
- Light Green Squares x 35
- Light Gray Squares x 18
- Dark Gray Squares x 18
- Light Blue Squares x 2
- Brown Squares x 24
- Black Squares x 7
- Dark Green Squares x 788

2" × 12½" (5.1 × 31.8cm) unfinished:

- Burgundy Strips x 60

3" × 3" (7.6 × 7.6cm) unfinished:

- White Squares x 75
- Gold Squares x 46
- Bright Red Squares x 71
- Burgundy Squares x 18
- Light Green Squares x 65
- Light Gray Squares x 24
- Dark Gray Squares x 29
- Light Blue Squares x 11
- Brown Squares x 12
- Black Squares x 1
- Dark Green Squares x 116

Making Half-Square Triangles

In this book, we'll use the two-at-a-time method to make half-square triangles (HSTs). It's quick, accurate, and perfect for building a rhythm as you sew.

1. Gather the 3" × 3" (7.6 × 7.6cm) squares (see page 15).
2. Take two different colors of fabric squares (see the checklist below) and place right sides together.
3. Draw a diagonal line on the wrong side of one of the squares.
4. Sew ¼" (6.4mm) away from the drawn line.
5. Turn the squares around. Sew another ¼" (6.4mm) away from the drawn line, so the stitching runs parallel.
6. With a rotary cutter, cut along the original drawn line.
7. Open each piece and press.
8. Trim so each piece is 2" × 2" (5.1 × 5.1cm) square.

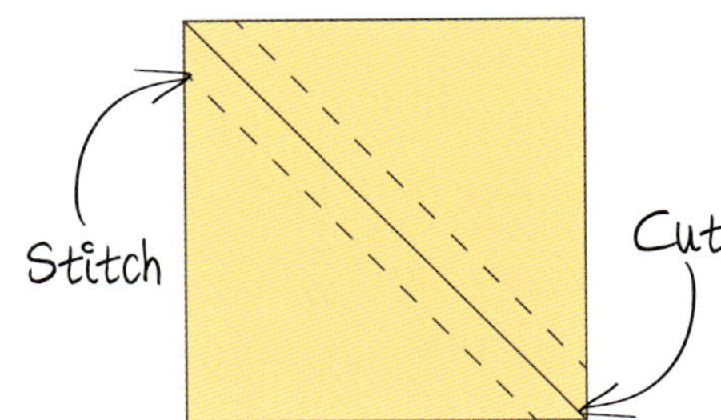

To make the HSTs, sew together the following:

- Dark Green and White x 23
- Dark Green and Light Green x 28
- Dark Green and Light Blue x 7
- Dark Green and Bright Red x 20
- Dark Green and Gold x 20
- Dark Green and Light Gray x 4
- Dark Green and Dark Gray x 9
- Dark Green and Brown x 3
- Dark Green and Burgundy x 1
- Dark Green and Black x 1
- Burgundy and Gold x 2
- Burgundy and Light Green x 6
- Burgundy and Bright Red x 9
- Light Green and Gold x 1
- Bright Red and Light Gray x 2
- Bright Red and Dark Gray x 3
- Bright Red and White x 12
- Bright Red and Light Green x 16
- Bright Red and Gold x 9
- Dark Gray and White x 2
- Dark Gray and Gold x 1
- Light Gray and Gold x 3
- Light Gray and Dark Gray x 14
- Light Gray and White x 1
- Brown and White x 9
- Light Blue and White x 4
- White and Gold x 10
- Light Green and White x 14

LEFTOVER HSTS

There will be one each of the following HSTs left over:

- Dark Green and White x 1 ☐
- Dark Green and Dark Gray x 1 ☐
- Dark Green and Brown x 1 ☐
- Bright Red and Dark Gray x 1 ☐
- Bright Red and White x 1 ☐
- Dark Gray and Gold x 1 ☐
- Light Gray and Gold x 1 ☐
- Brown and White x 1 ☐
- Light Green and White x 1 ☐

Check off when set aside

Joining Binding Strips

To create continuous binding, I join my 2½" (6.4cm) x WOF strips using a diagonal seam. This method reduces bulk, helps the binding flow smoothly around corners, and creates a neat, continuous binding with seams that are staggered and less noticeable on the finished quilt.

1. Lay two strips right sides together at a 90-degree angle, forming an L shape.
2. Draw a diagonal line from the top-left to the bottom-right corner of the overlap.
3. Sew along the line then trim the excess fabric, leaving a ¼" (6.4mm) seam allowance.
4. Press the seam open to reduce bulk.
5. Repeat until all strips are joined into one long binding strip.

Tip

If you're using directional prints or stripes, take care to align the pattern before sewing.

Pressing the Binding

Once all your binding strips are joined into one continuous length, it's time to prepare it for later use.

1. Start with the first end of the binding strip. Fold it in at a 90-degree angle to create a neat starting point; this will help when you join the ends later.
2. Fold the entire binding strip in half lengthwise, wrong sides together.
3. Press carefully along the full length, keeping the edges aligned. This creates a double-fold binding that's easy to apply and gives a clean, durable finish.

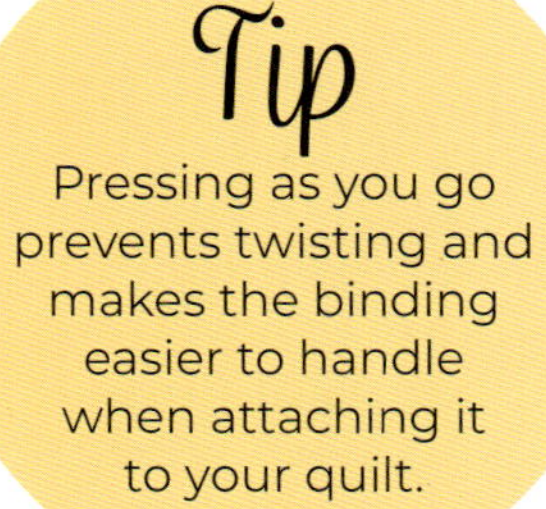

SEASONAL Quilt Blocks

This quilt is made up of 25 seasonal blocks, and you can use them in whatever way works best for you. I've shown you the layout I used, but you don't have to follow it. Feel free to move things around, repeat the blocks you enjoy most, or leave out anything that doesn't fit your color palette.

Think of this section as a set of building blocks rather than a fixed plan. You can keep things simple, go bold with your colors, or mix in fabrics from your own stash. There's plenty of room to make the quilt feel personal, and I hope you have fun experimenting as you go.

Remember

These blocks can be worked in different colors and prints to make them your own. Many can even be adapted for quilts not related to Christmas! For example, the "tomte"-style gnomes could be turned into garden gnomes or be adapted to another holiday.

Check off when completed

BLOCK 1:
SNOWY TREE
ROW BY ROW

Row 1: 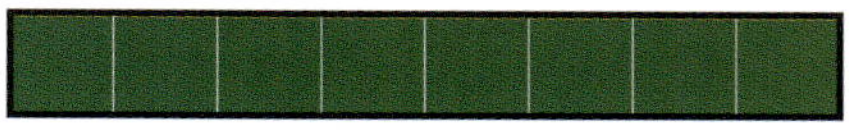 X 8

Row 2: X 6, X 2

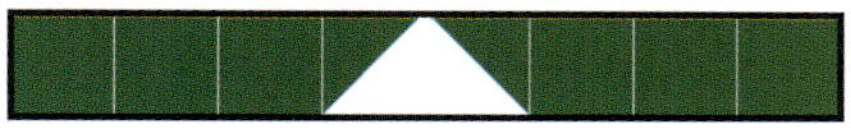

Row 3: X 4, X 2, X 2

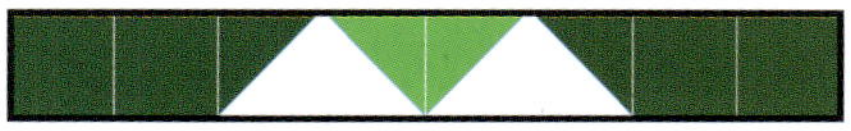

Row 4: X 4, X 2, X 2

Row 5: X 2, X 2, X 4

Row 6: X 2, X 4, X 2

Row 7: X 2, X 6

Row 8: X 6, X 2

BLOCK 2:
CANDIES
ROW BY ROW

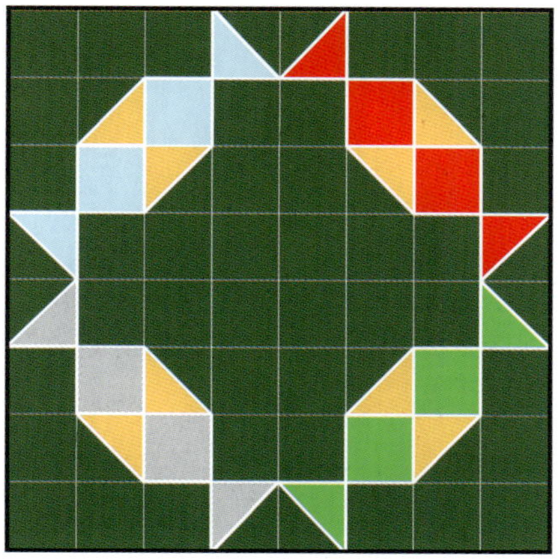

Row 1:  X 6, X 1, X 1

Row 2: X 4, X 1, X 1, X 2

Row 3: X 4, X 1, X 1, X 2

Row 4: X 6, X 1, X 1

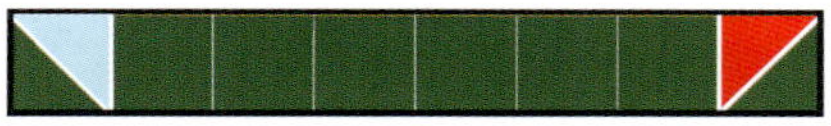

Row 5: X 6, X 1, X 1

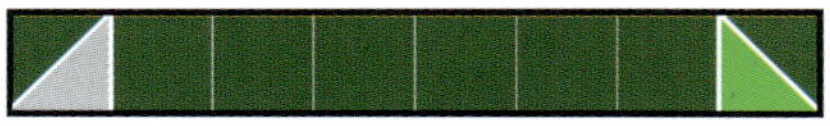

Row 6: X 4, X 1, X 1, X 2

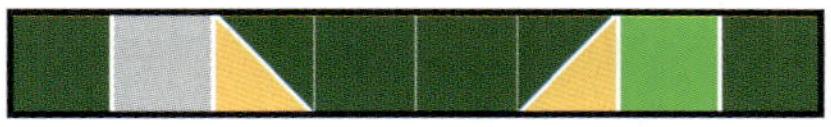

Row 7: X 4, X 1, X 1, X 2

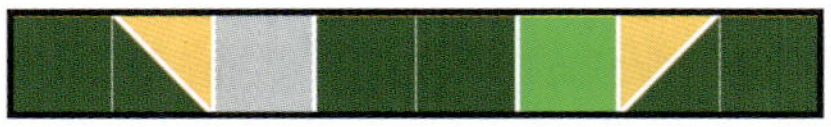

Row 8: X 6, X 1, X 1

BLOCK 3: CANDY CANE

ROW BY ROW

Row 1:  X 8

Row 2: X 4 X 1 X 2 X 1

Row 3: X 6 X 2

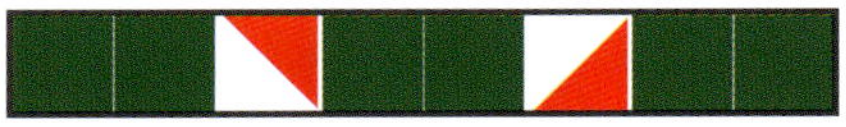

Row 4: X 7 X 1

Row 5: X 7 X 1

Row 6: X 7 X 1

Row 7: X 7 X 1

Row 8: X 8

BLOCK 4: CHRISTMAS CRACKER

ROW BY ROW

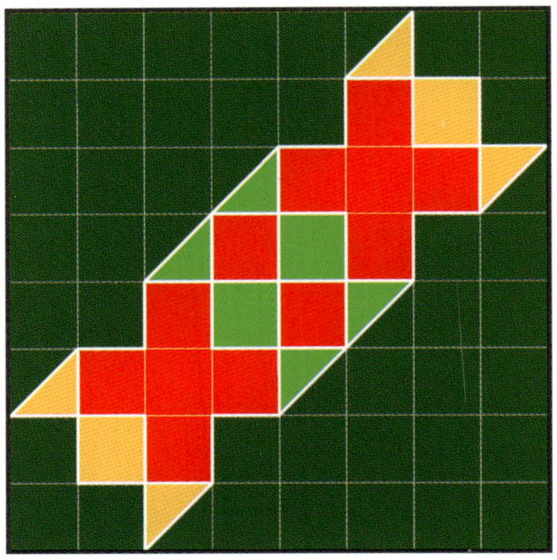

Row 1:  X 7 X 1

Row 2: X 6 X 1 X 1

Row 3: X 3 X 3 X 1 X 1

Row 4: X 4 X 2 X 1 X 1

Row 5: X 4 X 2 X 1 X 1

Row 6: X 3 X 3 X 1 X 1

Row 7: X 6 X 1 X 1

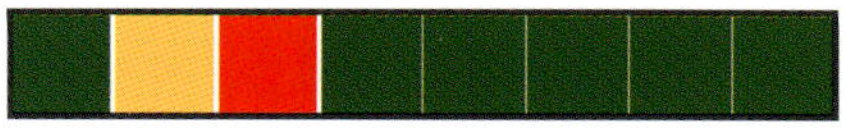

Row 8: X 7 X 1

BLOCK 5:
ORNAMENT A
ROW BY ROW

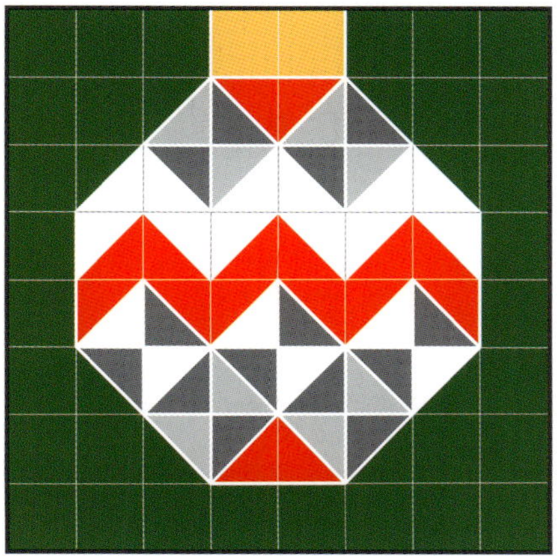

Row 1: X 6, X 2

Row 2: X 4, X 1, X 1, X 1, X 1

Row 3: X 2, X 2, X 2, X 2

Row 4: X 2, X 6

Row 5: X 2, X 3, X 3

Row 6: X 2, X 1, X 1, X 2, X 2

Row 7: X 4, X 1, X 1, X 1, X 1

Row 8: X 8

BLOCK 6:
CHRISTMAS BELL
ROW BY ROW

Row 1: X 8

Row 2: X 4, X 2, X 2

Row 3: X 4, X 4

Row 4: X 4, X 4

Row 5: X 2, X 2, X 4

Row 6: X 2, X 6

Row 7: X 7, X 1

Row 8: X 8

BLOCK 7:
SANTA HAT
ROW BY ROW

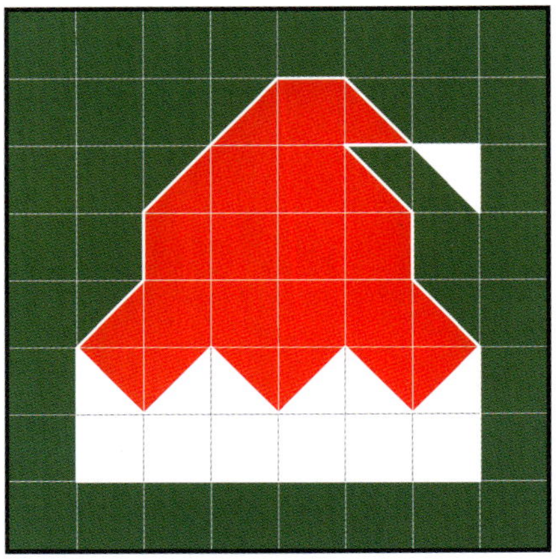

Row 1: 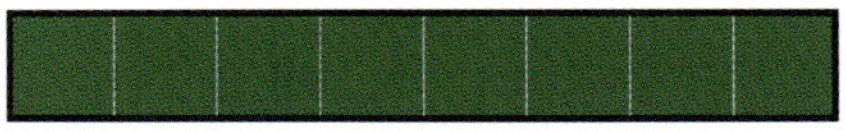 X 8

Row 2: X 5 X 1 X 2

Row 3: X 3 X 2 X 2 X 1

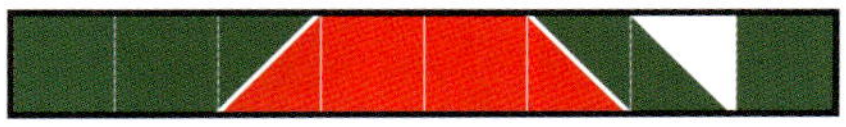

Row 4: X 4 X 4

Row 5: X 2 X 4 X 2

Row 6: X 2 X 6

Row 7: X 2 X 6

Row 8: X 8

BLOCK 8:
CANDLES A
ROW BY ROW

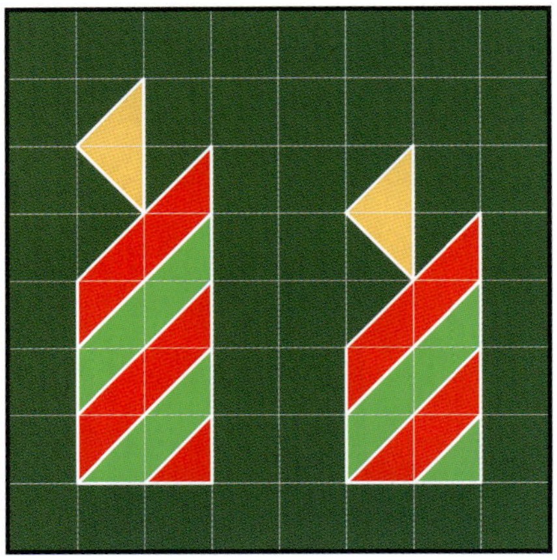

Row 1: 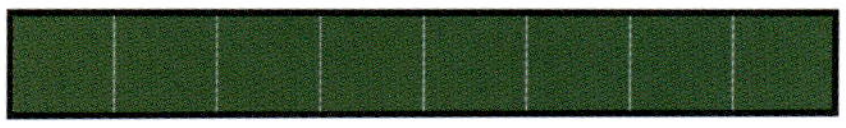 X 8

Row 2: X 7 X 1

Row 3: X 5 X 2 X 1

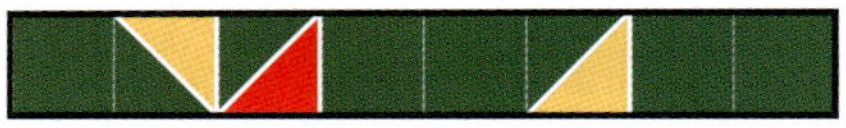

Row 4: X 4 X 1 X 2 X 1

Row 5: X 4 X 4

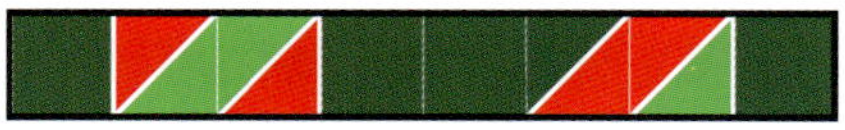

Row 6: X 4 X 4

Row 7: X 4 X 4

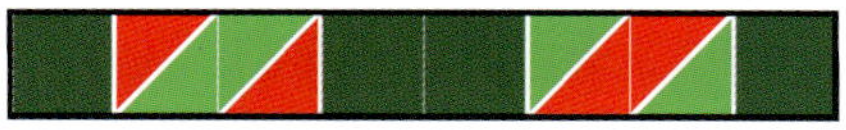

Row 8: X 8

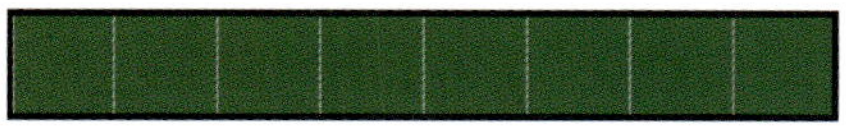

BLOCK 9:
SMALL HOUSE
ROW BY ROW

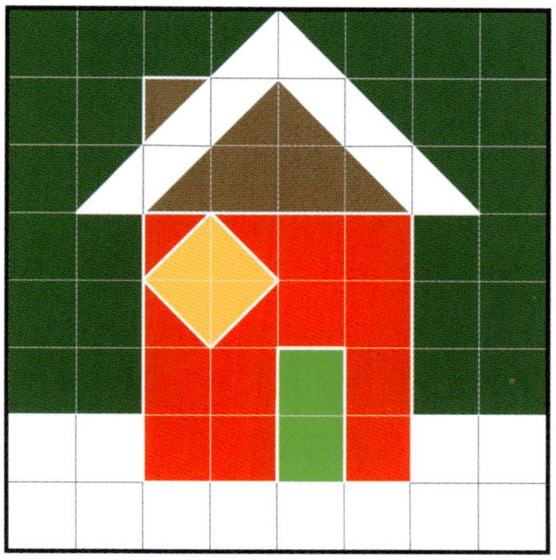

Row 1: 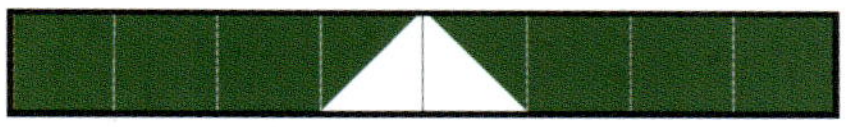 X 6 X 2

Row 2: X 4 X 1 X 3

Row 3: X 2 X 2 X 2 X 2

Row 4: X 4 X 2 X 2

Row 5: X 4 X 2 X 2

Row 6: X 4 X 3 X 1

Row 7: X 4 X 3 X 1

Row 8: X 8

BLOCK 10:
CHRISTMAS TREE
ROW BY ROW

Row 1:  X 8

Row 2: X 6 X 2

Row 3: X 4 X 2 X 2

Row 4: X 4 X 2 X 2

Row 5: X 2 X 4 X 2

Row 6: X 2 X 4 X 2

Row 7: X 6 X 2

Row 8: X 6 X 2

BLOCK 11:
BIG HOUSE
ROW BY ROW

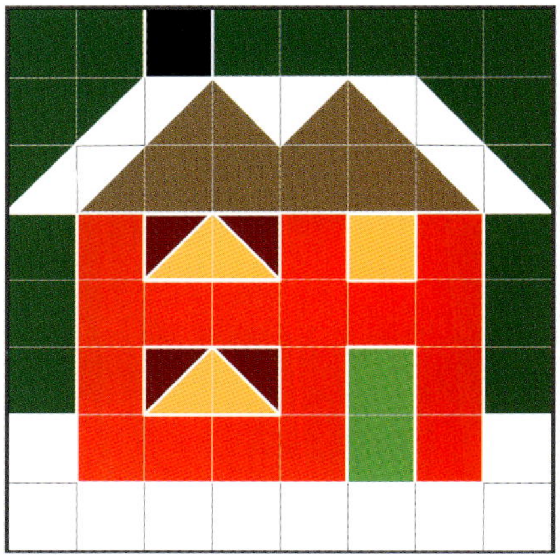

Row 1:
X 7 X 1 

Row 2: 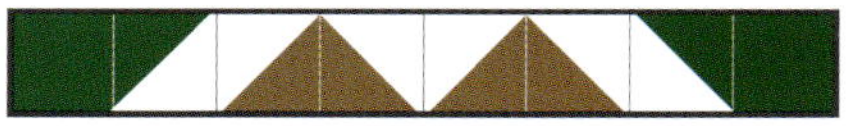
X 2 X 2 X 4

Row 3: 
X 4 X 2 X 2

Row 4: 
X 2 X 3 X 1 X 2

Row 5: 
X 2 X 6

Row 6: 
X 2 X 3 X 1 X 2

Row 7: 
X 2 X 5 X 1

Row 8: 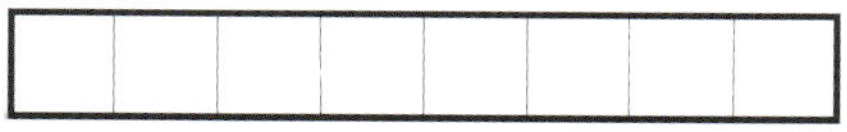
X 8

BLOCK 12:
WREATH
ROW BY ROW

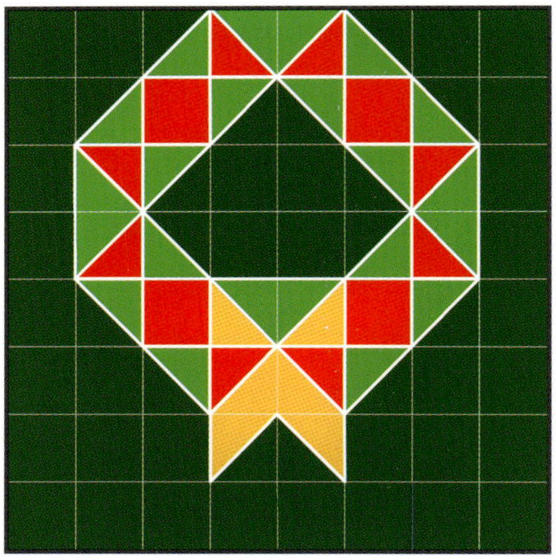

Row 1:
X 4 X 2 X 2 

Row 2: 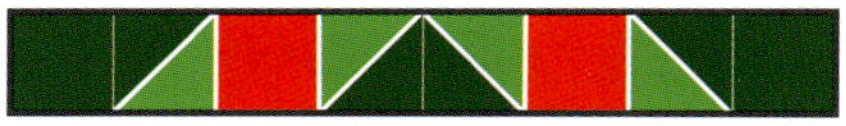
X 2 X 2 X 4

Row 3: 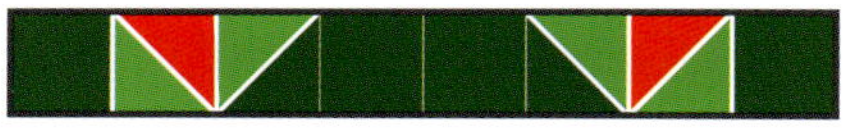
X 4 X 2 X 2

Row 4: 
X 4 X 2 X 2

Row 5: 
X 2 X 2 X 2 X 2

Row 6: 
X 4 X 2 X 2

Row 7: 
X 6 X 2

Row 8: 
X 8

BLOCK 13:
SNOWFLAKE
ROW BY ROW

Row 1:

X 8

Row 2:

X 4 X 3 X 1

Row 3:

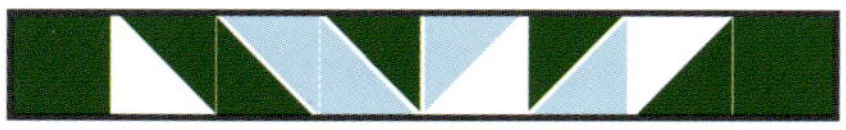

X 2 X 2 X 3 X 1

Row 4:

X 2 X 1 X 2 X 3

Row 5:

X 2 X 1 X 2 X 3

Row 6:

X 2 X 2 X 3 X 1

Row 7:

X 4 X 3 X 1

Row 8:

X 8

BLOCK 14:
CHRISTMAS PUDDING
ROW BY ROW

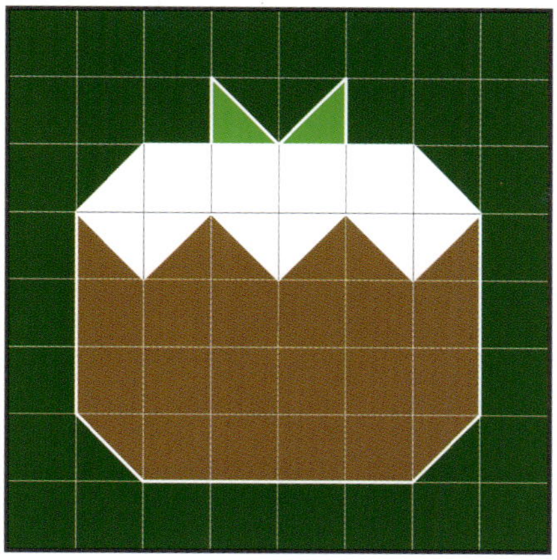

Row 1:

X 8

Row 2:

X 6 X 2

Row 3:

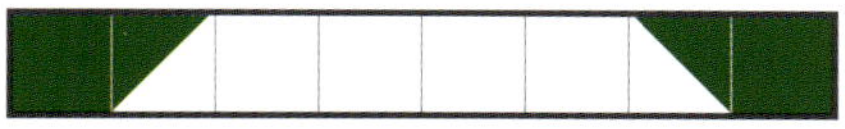

X 2 X 4 X 2

Row 4:

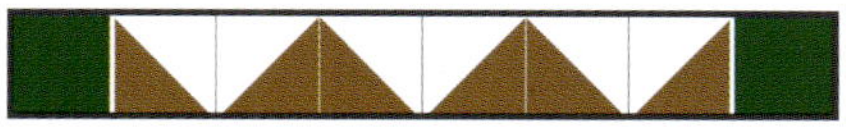

X 2 X 6

Row 5:

X 2 X 6

Row 6:

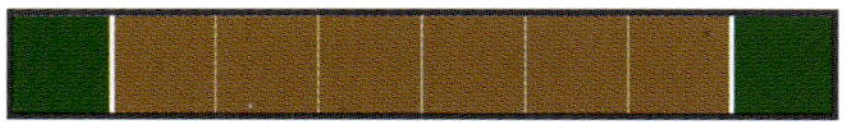

X 2 X 6

Row 7:

X 2 X 4 X 2

Row 8:

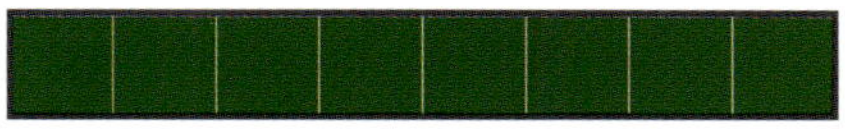

X 8

BLOCK 15:
CHRISTMAS GNOME A
ROW BY ROW

Row 1:  X 5, X 1, X 2

Row 2: X 3, X 3, X 2

Row 3: X 3, X 4, X 1

Row 4: X 2, X 4, X 2

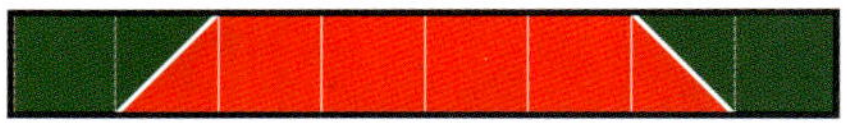

Row 5: X 4, X 2, X 2

Row 6: X 2, X 2, X 2, X 2

Row 7: X 4, X 2, X 2

Row 8: X 2, X 2, X 2, X 2

BLOCK 16:
CHRISTMAS STOCKING
ROW BY ROW

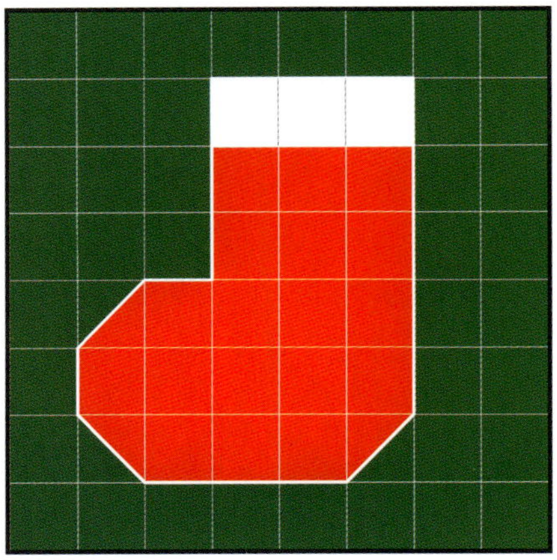

Row 1:  X 8

Row 2: X 5, X 3

Row 3: X 5, X 3

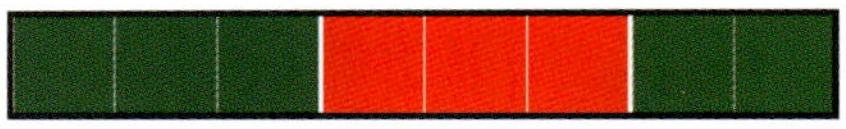

Row 4: X 5, X 3

Row 5: X 3, X 4, X 1

Row 6: X 3, X 5

Row 7: X 3, X 3, X 2

Row 8: X 8

BLOCK 17: GIFT TAG

ROW BY ROW

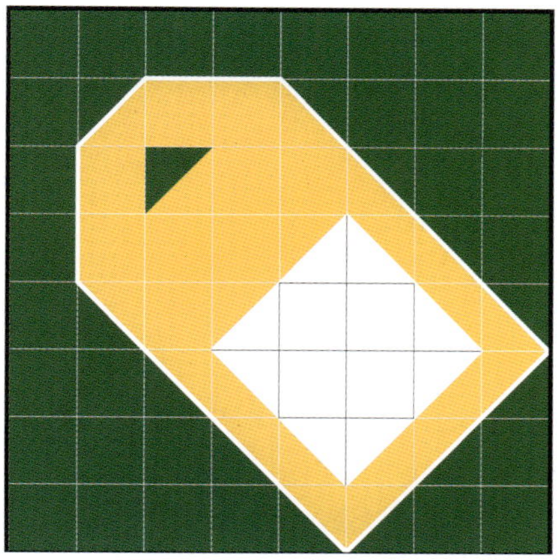

Row 1:  X 8

Row 2: X 4 X 2 X 2

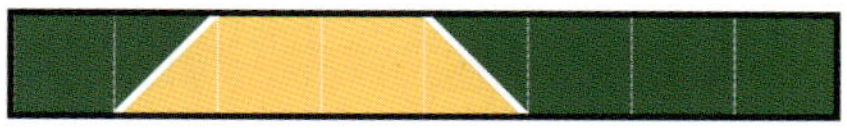

Row 3: X 3 X 3 X 2

Row 4: X 2 X 3 X 1 X 2

Row 5: X 1 X 1 X 2 X 2 X 2

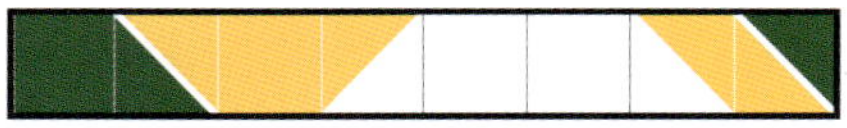

Row 6: X 2 X 2 X 2 X 2

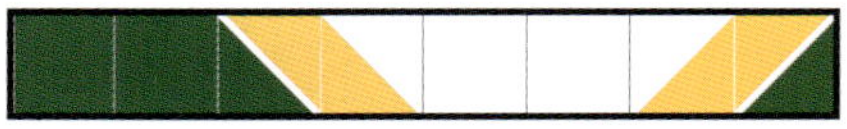

Row 7: X 4 X 2 X 2

Row 8: X 6 X 2

BLOCK 18: ORNAMENT B

ROW BY ROW

Row 1:  X 6 X 2

Row 2: X 4 X 2 X 2

Row 3: X 2 X 2 X 4

Row 4: X 2 X 6

Row 5: X 2 X 6

Row 6: X 2 X 2 X 4

Row 7: X 4 X 2 X 2

Row 8: X 8

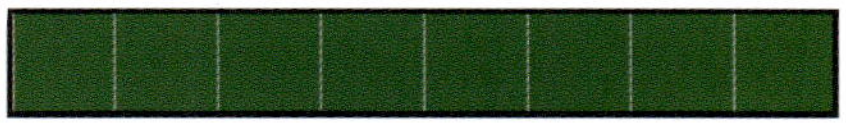

BLOCK 19:
KNIT HAT
ROW BY ROW

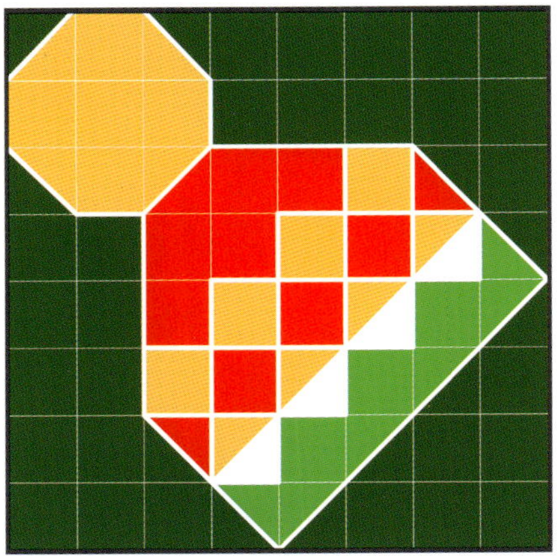

Row 1:  X 5 X 1 X 2

Row 2: X 5 X 3

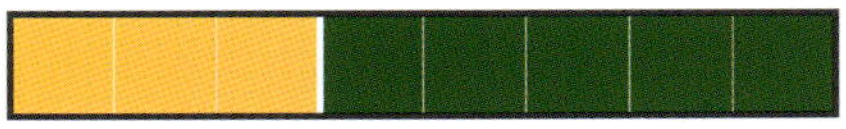

Row 3: X 1 X 2 X 2 X 1 X 1 X 1

Row 4: X 2 X 3 X 1 X 1 X 1

Row 5: X 2 X 2 X 1 X 1 X 1 X 1

Row 6: X 3 X 1 X 1 X 1 X 1 X 1

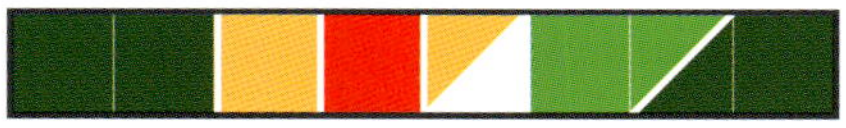

Row 7: X 4 X 1 X 1 X 1 X 1

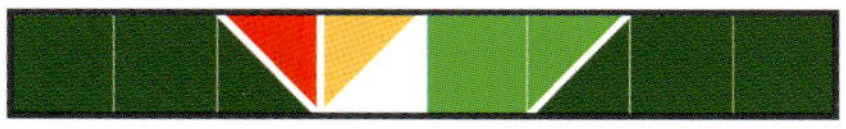

Row 8: X 6 X 2

BLOCK 20:
CANDLES B
ROW BY ROW

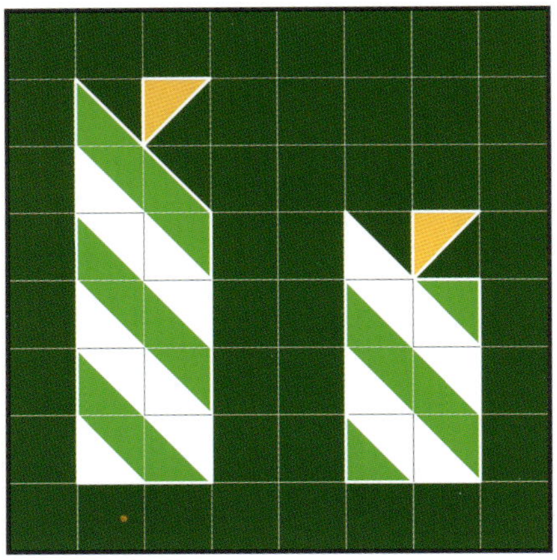

Row 1: 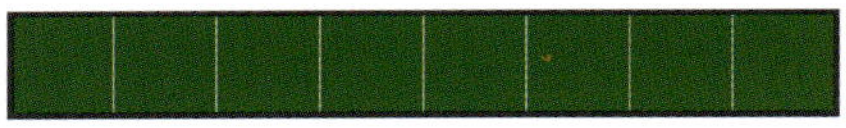 X 8

Row 2: X 6 X 1 X 1

Row 3: X 6 X 1 X 1

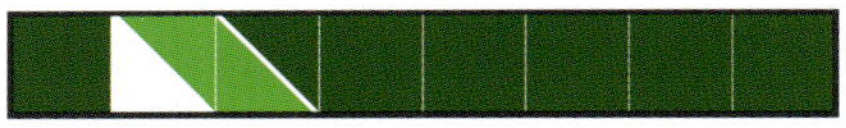

Row 4: X 4 X 2 X 1 X 1

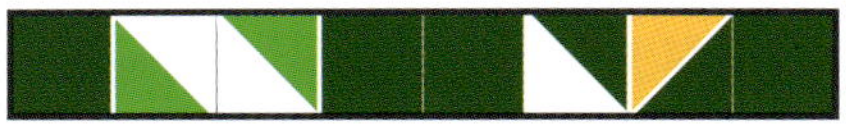

Row 5: X 4 X 4

Row 6: X 4 X 4

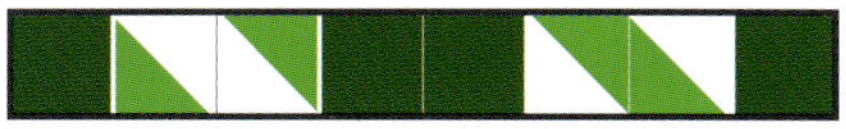

Row 7: X 4 X 4

Row 8: X 8

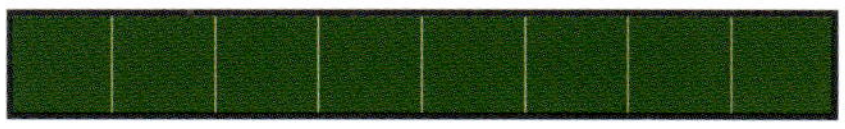

BLOCK 21:
PRESENT
ROW BY ROW

Row 1:  X 6, X 2

Row 2: X 4, X 2, X 2

Row 3: X 2, X 2, X 2, X 2

Row 4: X 6, X 2

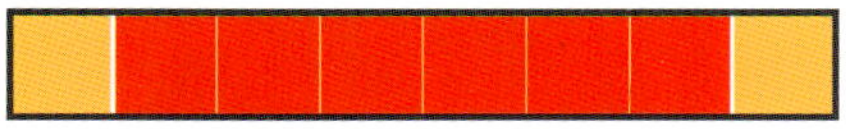

Row 5: X 6, X 2

Row 6: X 2, X 2, X 2, X 2

Row 7: X 4, X 2, X 2

Row 8: X 6, X 2

BLOCK 22:
CHRISTMAS GNOME B
ROW BY ROW

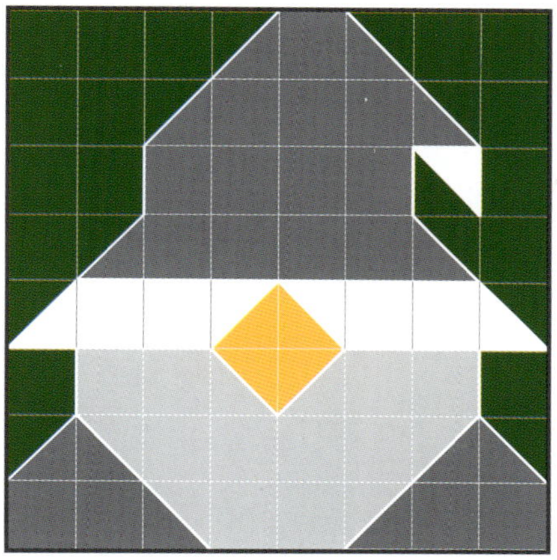

Row 1:  X 5, X 1, X 2

Row 2: X 3, X 3, X 2

Row 3: X 3, X 4, X 1

Row 4: X 2, X 4, X 2

Row 5: X 4, X 2, X 2

Row 6: X 2, X 4, X 2

Row 7: X 4, X 2, X 2

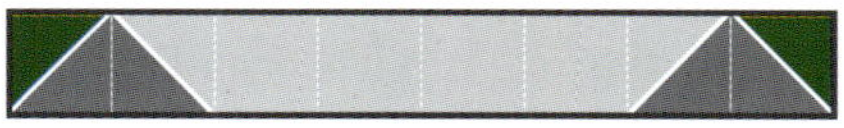

Row 8: X 4, X 2, X 2

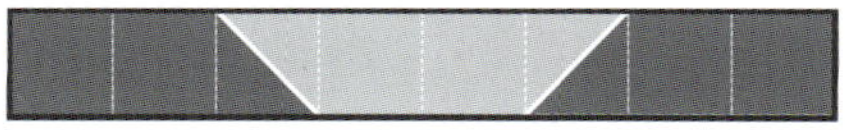

BLOCK 23:
MAILBOX
ROW BY ROW

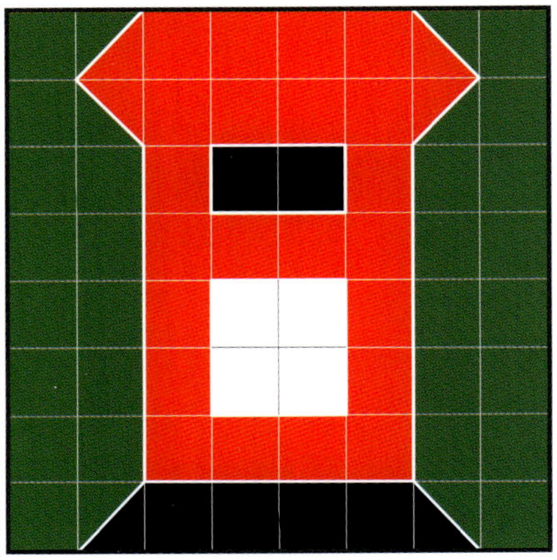

Row 1: 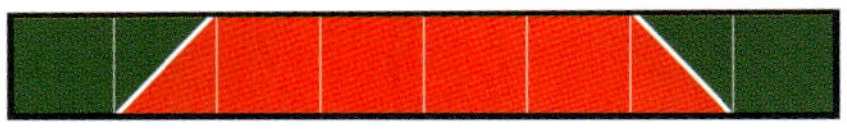 X 2 X 4 X 2

Row 2: X 2 X 4 X 2

Row 3: X 4 X 2 X 2

Row 4: X 4 X 4

Row 5: X 4 X 2 X 2

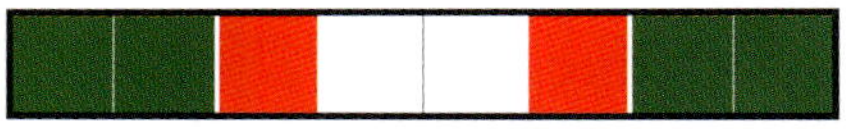

Row 6: X 4 X 2 X 2

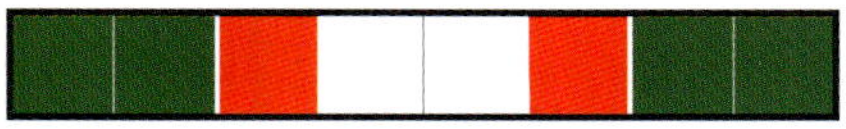

Row 7: X 4 X 4

Row 8: X 2 X 4 X 2

BLOCK 24:
ORNAMENT C
ROW BY ROW

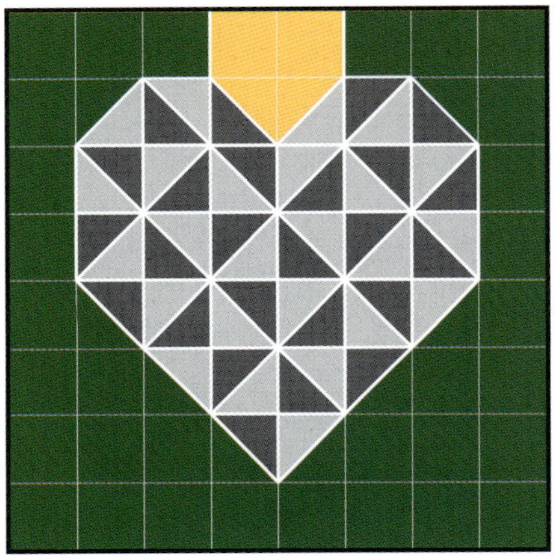

Row 1:  X 6 X 2

Row 2: X 2 X 1 X 1 X 2 X 1 X 1

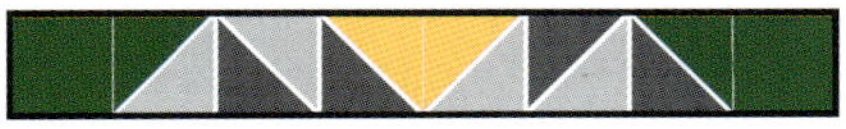

Row 3: X 2 X 6

Row 4: X 2 X 6

Row 5: X 2 X 1 X 1 X 4

Row 6: X 4 X 1 X 1 X 2

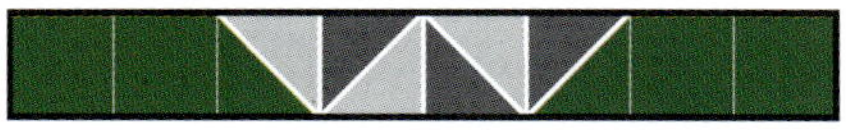

Row 7: X 6 X 1 X 1

Row 8: X 8

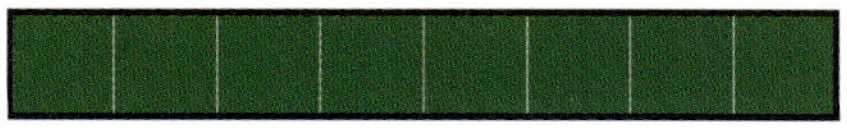

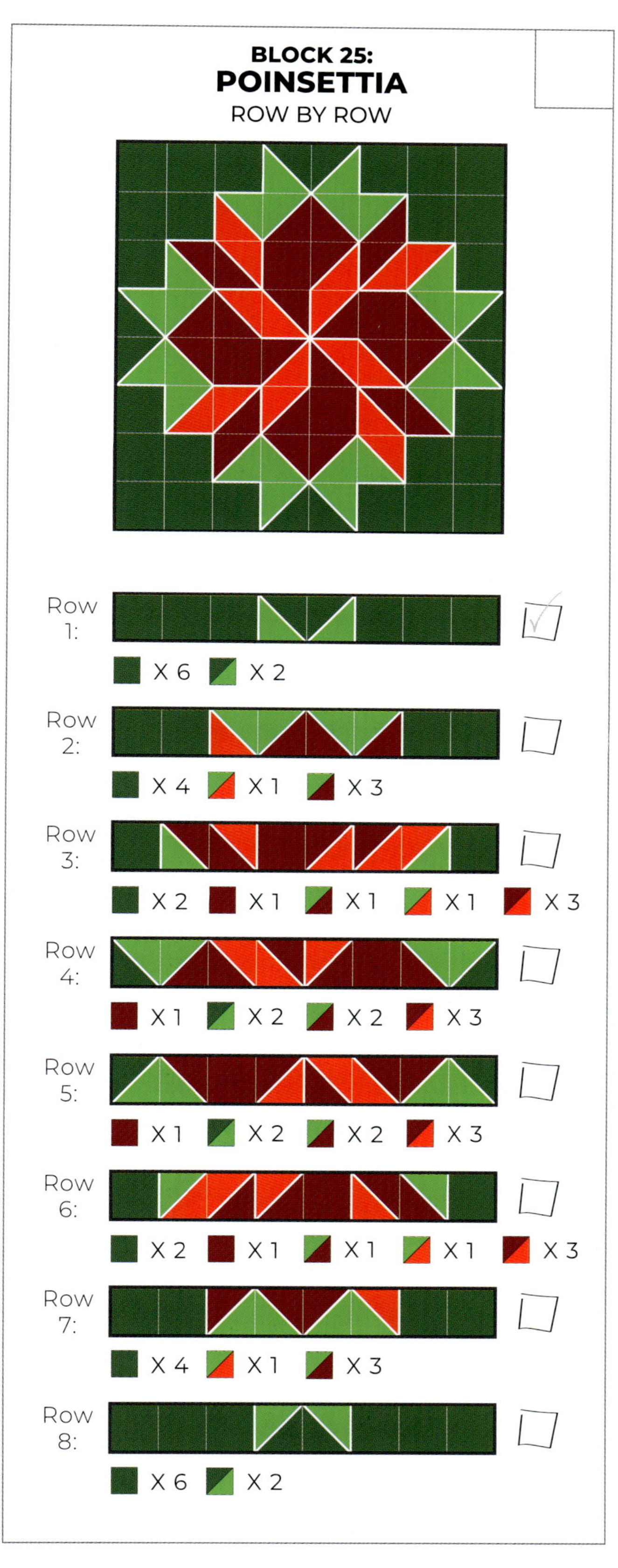
BLOCK 25:
POINSETTIA
ROW BY ROW
Row 1:
X 6
X 2
Row 2:
X 4
X 1
X 3
Row 3:
X 2
X 1
X 1
X 1
X 3
Row 4:
X 1
X 2
X 2
X 3
Row 5:
X 1
X 2
X 2
X 3
Row 6:
X 2
X 1
X 1
X 1
X 3
Row 7:
X 4
X 1
X 3
Row 8:
X 6
X 2

QUILT *Assembly*

You will need the following:

- 2" × 2" (5.1 × 5.1cm) Gold Squares **x 36** ☑
- 2" × 12½" (5.1 × 31.8cm) Burgundy Strips **x 30** ☐
- 12½" × 12½" (31.8 × 31.8cm) Blocks **x 25** ☐

BLOCKS, SASHING & CORNERSTONES

1. Sew together six Gold Cornerstones and five Burgundy Sashing Strips, as per the diagram below. Use a ¼" (6.4mm) seam allowance.
2. Repeat to make six Sashing and Cornerstones Rows. Press the seam allowance inward, toward the gold. Do this for each Gold Cornerstone.
3. Sew together the 25 Christmas Blocks following the diagrams below and on the opposite page. Use a ¼" (6.4mm) seam allowance.

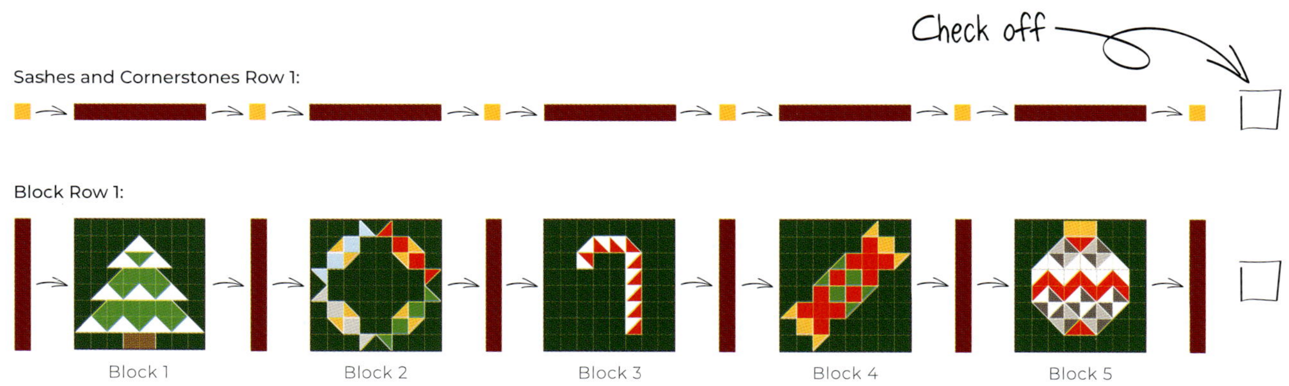

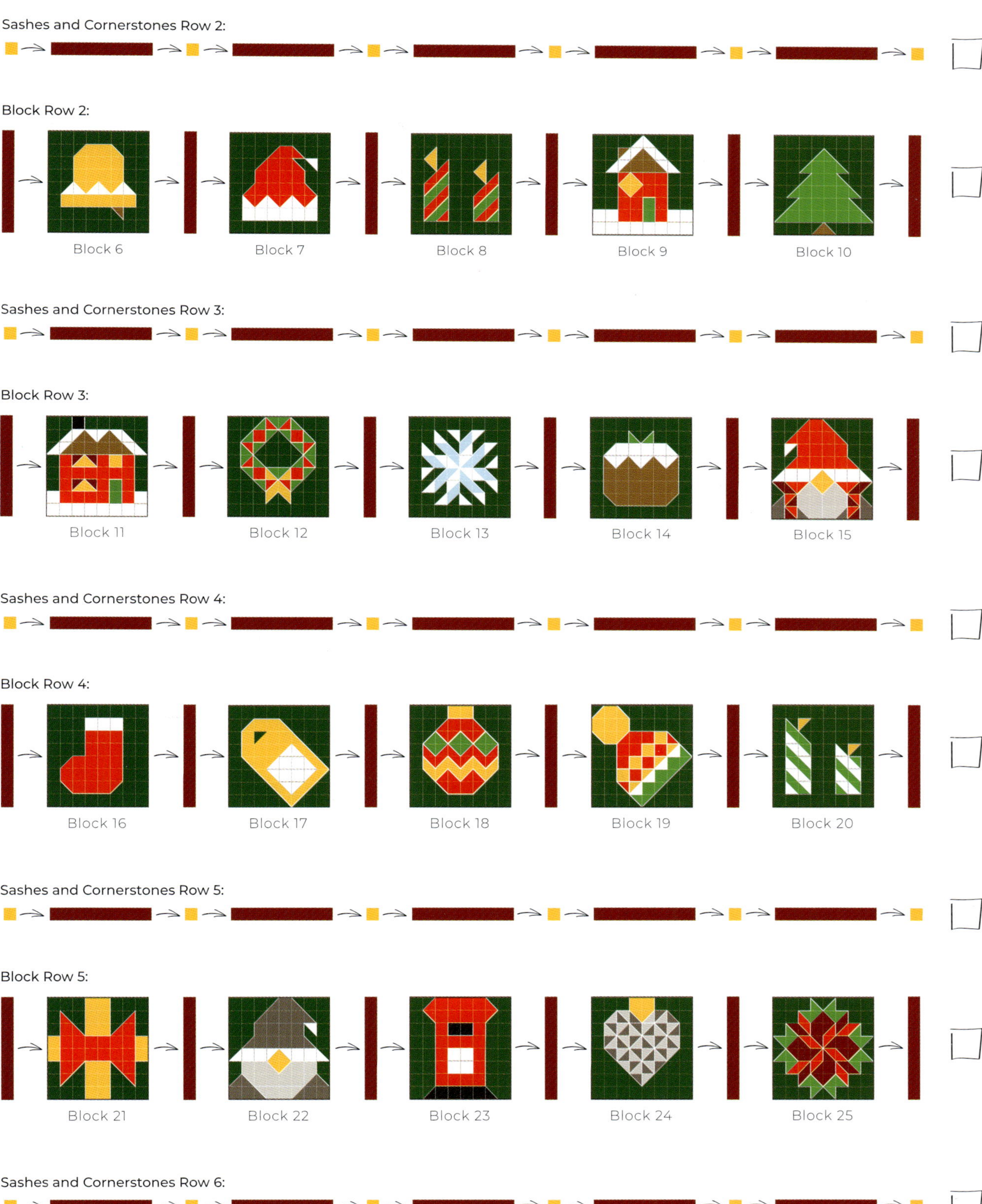
Sashes and Cornerstones Row 2:
Block Row 2:
Block 6
Block 7
Block 8
Block 9
Block 10
Sashes and Cornerstones Row 3:
Block Row 3:
Block 11
Block 12
Block 13
Block 14
Block 15
Sashes and Cornerstones Row 4:
Block Row 4:
Block 16
Block 17
Block 18
Block 19
Block 20
Sashes and Cornerstones Row 5:
Block Row 5:
Block 21
Block 22
Block 23
Block 24
Block 25
Sashes and Cornerstones Row 6:

ROW BY ROW

1. Press the Blocks, this time pressing the seam allowance outward toward the Blocks. By doing this, when you sew the Sashing and Cornerstones Rows to the Block Rows, you will be able to nest those rows nicely together.
2. Optionally, pin the Sashing and Cornerstone Rows to the Block Rows for further accuracy before sewing together.
3. Sew together the six Sashing and Cornerstone Rows and five Block Rows to complete the quilt top.

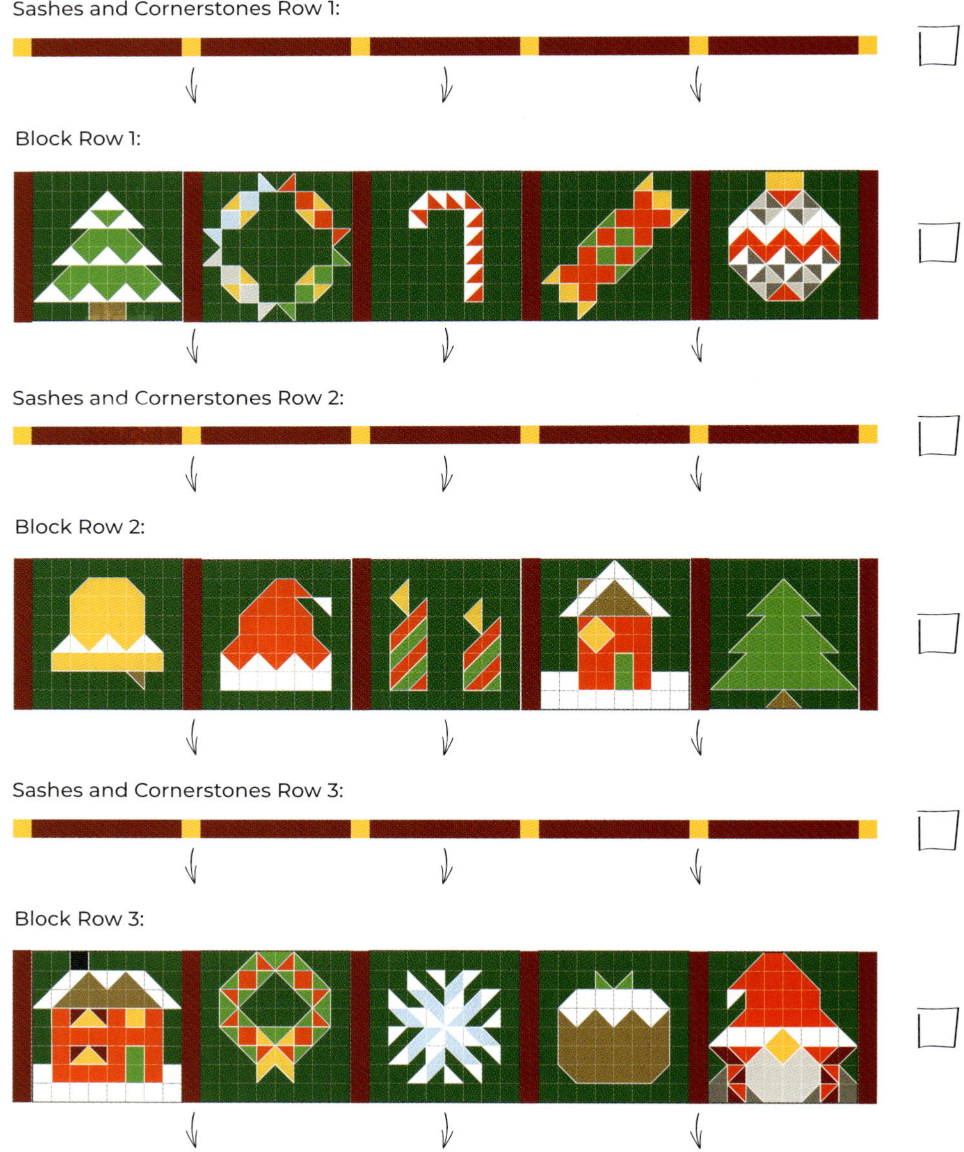

MEGA CHRISTMAS QUILT

After sewing together the rows, layer the quilt top, batting, and backing. Quilt and bind using your preferred method. Your completed 73" × 73" (185.4 × 185.4cm) quilt will look like this.

FESTIVE Mini Projects

This section brings together three smaller makes: the table runner, the lap quilt, and the cushion cover. They're quick, practical projects that let you add a bit of seasonal color to your home without committing to a full quilt.

Each project is simple to customize, whether you want to change the colors, adjust the size, or use fabrics you already have. You can make them as matching pieces or treat them as standalone projects—whatever suits your space and your style.

They're designed to be enjoyable, approachable pieces for the festive season, and I hope you have fun putting your own spin on them.

Christmas Pudding Lap Quilt

Measuring 40" × 40" (101.6 × 101.6cm), this festive lap quilt is the perfect seasonal project to brighten your home. Inspired by the cozy tradition of Christmas pudding, a classic British dessert served at Christmas for generations, this design captures the warmth and nostalgia of the season. It's a simple quilt to make and ideal for beginners or for anyone looking for a joyful, low-stress project during the busy holiday period. Whether draped over a chair, gifted to a loved one, or used to add a touch of cheer to your winter evenings, this quilt is as delightful to sew as it is to enjoy.

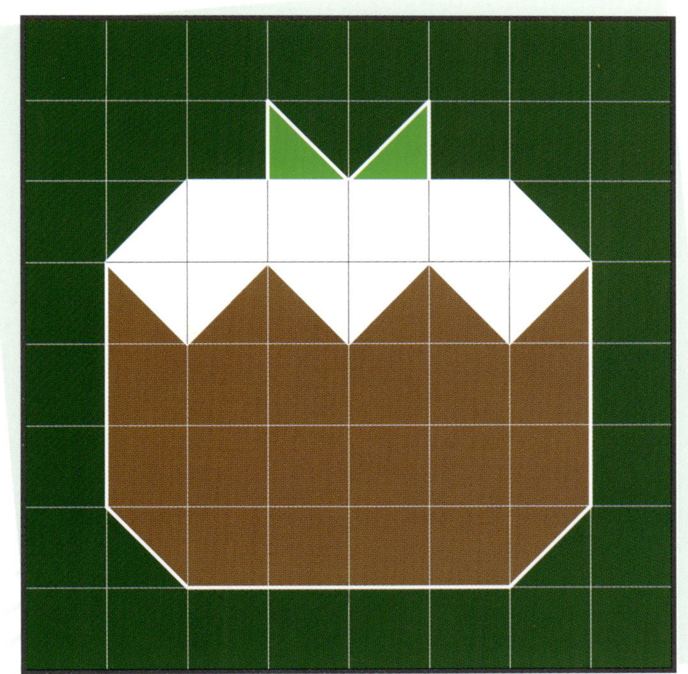

Check off

FABRIC REQUIREMENTS:

- 1 yard (91.4cm) Dark Green ☐
- ½ yard (45.7cm) White ☐
- ¾ yard (68.6cm) Brown ☐
- ¼ yard (22.9cm) Light Green ☐
- 44" × 44" (111.8 × 111.8cm) Batting ☐
- 42" (106.7cm) × WOF of Backing ☐
- 10" (25.4cm) × WOF of Binding ☐

CUT THE FOLLOWING:

5½" × 5½" (14 × 14cm) unfinished:

- Dark Green Squares x 32 ☑
- White Squares x 4 ☐
- Brown Squares x 16 ☐

6½" × 6½" (16.5 × 16.5cm) unfinished:

- Dark Green Squares x 3 ☐
- White Squares x 4 ☐
- Brown Squares x 4 ☐
- Light Green Squares x 1 ☐

SEW THE FOLLOWING:

- Light Green and Dark Green x 1 ☐
- Dark Green and White x 1 ☐
- Dark Green and Brown x 1 ☐
- White and Brown x 3 ☐

1. Using the 6½" × 6½" (16.5 × 16.5cm) squares, make the HSTs as listed. Refer to the Making Half-Square Triangles (page 16) for instructions; in step 8, trim to 5½" × 5½" (14 × 14cm) square.
2. Join the squares in rows according to Block 14: Christmas Pudding (page 25). All seams are sewn with a ¼" (6.4mm) seam allowance.
3. Layer the quilt top, batting, and backing. Quilt and bind using your preferred method.

Gift Tag Cushion Cover

This playful cushion cover is inspired by the charm of a classic gift tag, which gives a little nod to celebration and joy. Measuring 20" × 20" (50.8 × 50.8cm), it's a quick, creative make that adds a touch of fun to any room. The steps are simple and beginner-friendly, making it a lovely project for an afternoon of sewing.

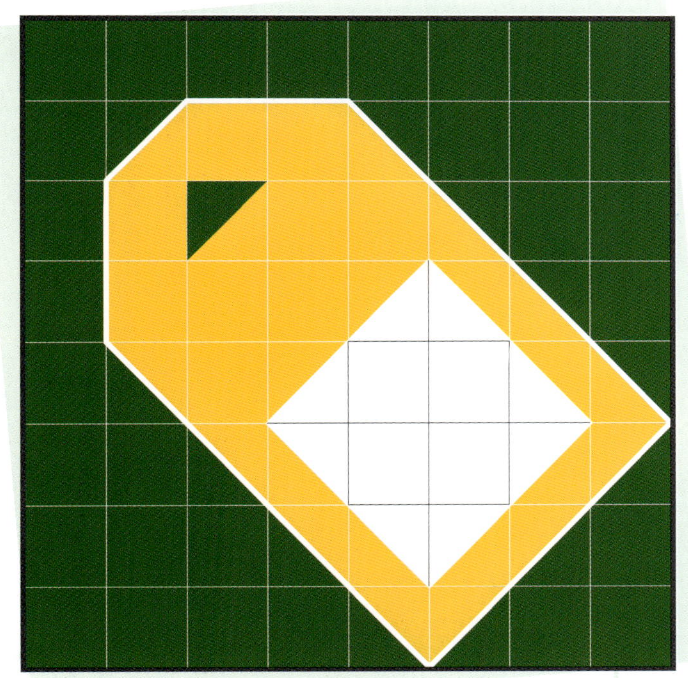

Check off

FABRIC REQUIREMENTS:

- ½ yard (45.7cm) Dark Green
- ½ yard (45.7cm) Yellow
- ¼ yard (22.9cm) White
- 24" × 24" (61 × 61cm) Batting
- 21" × 21" (53.3 × 53.3cm) Backing
- 26" × 20½" (66 × 52.1cm) Backing x 2

CUT THE FOLLOWING:

3" × 3" (7.6 × 7.6cm) unfinished:

- Dark Green Squares x 30
- Yellow Squares x 9
- White Squares x 4

4" × 4" (10.2 × 10.2cm) unfinished:

- Dark Green Squares x 7
- Yellow Squares x11
- White Squares x 4

SEW THE FOLLOWING:

- Dark Green and Yellow x 7
- White and Yellow x 4

You will have one Dark Green and Yellow HST left over.

1. Using the 4" × 4" (10.2 × 10.2cm) squares, make the HSTs as listed. Refer to the Making Half-Square Triangles (page 16) for instructions; in step 8, trim to 3" × 3" (7.6 × 7.6cm) square.
2. Join the squares in rows according to Block 17: Gift Tag (page 27). All seams are sewn with a ¼" (6.4mm) seam allowance.
3. Layer the cushion top, batting, and 21" × 21" (53.3 × 53.3cm) backing. Quilt and trim to 20½" × 20½" (52.1 × 52.1cm) square.
4. Place one 26" × 20½" (66 × 52.1cm) backing fabric right side down, with the 26" (66cm) measurement at the top and bottom and the 20½" (52.1cm) measurement at the sides.
5. Fold the backing in half, wrong sides together. It will measure 13" × 20½" (33 × 52.1cm). Press the fold line with an iron. Sew along the fold line with a ⅛" (3.2 mm) seam allowance or use a decorative stitch.
6. Repeat steps 4 and 5 for the second backing piece.
7. Place the quilted front panel right side up. Place both backing pieces on top, with the raw edges around the outside of the front panel and lined up with the sides. The backing fold lines will overlap on the inside by about 5½" (14cm).
8. Secure the backing and the front panel together with sewing clips or pins. Stitch around the whole cushion using a ¼" (6.4mm) seam allowance. Turn right side out, and you have a finished, enveloped-backed cushion cover.

Christmas Table Runner

Bring a little festive warmth to your table with this cheerful runner, sized 42" × 15" (106.7 × 38.1cm). It's a relaxed, approachable project designed to help beginners build confidence while creating something beautiful for their home. Whether you're decorating for the season or gifting it to someone special, this table runner comes together with ease.

Check off

FABRIC REQUIREMENTS:

- ½ yard (45.7cm) Navy
- ¼ yard (22.9cm) Brown
- ¼ yard (22.9cm) Light Green
- ¼ yard (22.9cm) White
- ¼ yard (22.9cm) Gold
- ¼ yard (22.9cm) Bright Red
- 46" × 19" (116.8 × 48.3cm) Batting
- 46" × 19" (116.8 × 48.3cm) Backing
- ¼ yard (22.9cm) Binding

CUT THE FOLLOWING:

2" × 2" (5.1 × 5.1cm) unfinished:

- Navy Squares x 120
- Brown Squares x 2
- Light Green Squares x 6
- Gold Squares x 8

3" × 3" (7.6 × 7.6cm) unfinished:

- Navy Squares x 14
- Light Green Squares x 20
- White Squares x 26
- Gold Squares x 4

2" × 12½" (5.1 × 31.8cm) unfinished:

- Bright Red Strips x 10

SEW THE FOLLOWING:

- Navy and Gold x 4
- Navy and White x 8
- Light Green and White x 18
- Navy and Light Green x 2

1. Using the 3" × 3" (7.6 × 7.6cm) squares, make the HSTs as listed. Refer to the Making Half-Square Triangles (page 16) for instructions.
2. Join the squares in rows according to Left Candles Block, Tree Block, and Right Candles Block (pages 43–44). All seams are sewn with a ¼" (6.4mm) seam allowance.

Instructions continued on page 44.

Check off when completed

LEFT CANDLES BLOCK
ROW BY ROW

Row 1:  X 8

Row 2: X 7 X 1

Row 3: X 5 X 2 X 1

Row 4: X 4 X 1 X 2 X 1

Row 5: X 4 X 1 X 3

Row 6: X 4 X 4

Row 7: X 4 X 4

Row 8: X 8

RIGHT CANDLES BLOCK
ROW BY ROW

Row 1: X 8

Row 2: X 7 X 1

Row 3: X 5 X 2 X 1

Row 4: X 4 X 1 X 2 X 1

Row 5: X 4 X 1 X 3

Row 6: X 4 X 4

Row 7: X 4 X 4

Row 8: X 8

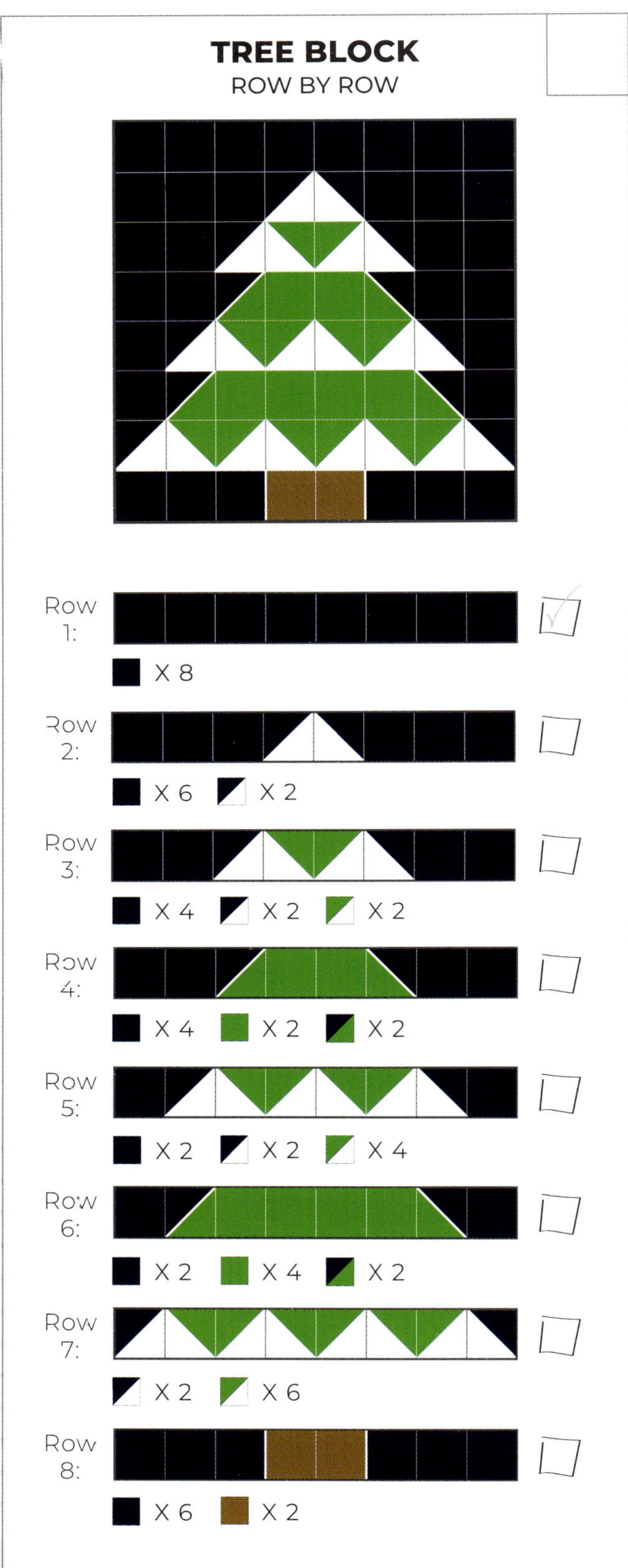

3. Sew together four Gold Cornerstones and three Bright Red Sashing Strips, as per the diagram on page 45.
4. Repeat to make a second Sashing and Cornerstones Row. Press the seam allowance inward, toward the gold. Do this for each Gold Cornerstone.
5. Sew together the three Christmas Table Runner Blocks following the diagram on page 45.
6. Press the Blocks, this time pressing the seam allowance outward toward the Blocks. By doing this, when you sew the Sashing and Cornerstones Rows to the Block Row, you will be able to nest those rows nicely together.
7. Optionally, pin the Sashing and Cornerstone Rows to the Block Row for further accuracy before sewing together.
8. Sew together the two Sashing and Cornerstone Rows and one Block Row to complete the table runner top.
9. Layer the table runner top, batting, and backing. Quilt and bind using your preferred method.

Check off
Sashes and Cornerstones Row 1:
Block Row:
Left Candles Block
Tree Block
Right Candles Block
Sashes and Cornerstones Row 2:
Sashes and Cornerstones Row 1:
Block Row:
Sashes and Cornerstones Row 2:

ABOUT the Author

Tracy Perks is a quilt pattern designer, retreat host, and creative business owner known for her seasonal designs and warm, community-focused approach. She runs her business from her floating narrowboat studio, The Little Boat, adapting her creative process to fit life on the water.

Whether she's designing a festive sampler, hosting a retreat, or appearing as a guest designer on the TV channel *Sewing Street*, Tracy brings clarity, warmth, and a deep love of making to everything she creates.

Her patterns are designed to be flexible and welcoming, with thoughtful details, clear instructions, and room for personal expression. She believes quilting should feel joyful, achievable, and full of meaning.

You can find Tracy online sharing tutorials, seasonal inspiration, and glimpses of narrowboat life with her growing community of quilters.

BIG *Thanks*

This project wouldn't exist without the love and encouragement of the people around me.

To Bri, Mr. Perks, my husband and greatest cheerleader, thank you for your unwavering belief in me. You encourage me in everything I do, even when I doubt myself, and your quiet confidence keeps me going.

To Donna, thank you for inspiring me to write this book and for your support throughout this project. Your encouragement helped bring this idea to life.

To my sister Lindsey, your constant belief in me means more than I can say. You've always been there, cheering me on.

To Lisa and Steve, thank you for the gentle nudges, the timely encouragement, and for always pointing me in the right direction.

To Lisa H., my graphic designer who gets my ideas into lovely illustrations.

To Adelle from PearPaw Quilting, who quilted the Mega Christmas Quilt for me.

To David, for letting me use the beautiful Hurds Hill Regency House for some of the photos.

I would like to thank Moda for providing the fabric for the Mega Christmas Quilt, using their beautiful Bella Solids Collection.

Finally, to the quilters who have supported me, bought my patterns, and shared their beautiful makes—thank you. Your creativity, kindness, and enthusiasm continue to inspire me every day.

With heartfelt thanks,

Tracy

INDEX